BY AIR MAIL
PAR AVION
U.S. POSTAGE
5¢
VIA AIR MAIL
U.S. POSTAGE
5¢
VIA AIR MAIL

AIRCRAFT

WARREN SINGER

REDBACK
publishing

First Published 2026 by
Redback Publishing
Suite 6, 13a Narabang Way,
Belrose NSW 2085
Australia

www.redbackpublishing.com
info@redbackpublishing.com

ISBN 978-1-761402-15-9

Author: Warren Singer
Editor: Simone Saba
Designer: Redback Publishing

Original illustrations © Redback Publishing 2026
Originated by Redback Publishing

Acknowledgements
Abbreviations: l—left, r—right, b—bottom, t—top, c—centre, m—middle
We would like to thank the following for permission to reproduce photographs: (Images © shutterstock)
p6ml - Flying Camera / Shutterstock.com, p7tr - User:Stahlkocher - Own work, CC BY-SA 3.0, https://commons.wikimedia.org/w/indexphp?curid=1274953, p7b - MikeDotta / Shutterstock.com, p8t - By Alert5 - commons.wikimedia, CC BY-SA 4.0, https://commons.wikimedia.org/w/index.php?curid=89389680, p8m - Soos Jozsef / Shutterstock.com, p8bl - USAF - https://www.dvidshub.net/image/8423170/b-21-raider-continues-flight-test-production, Public Domain, https://commons.wikimedia.org/w/index.php?curid=148631292, p9tl - rikinik / Shutterstock.com, p9m - Angel DiBilio / Shutterstock.com, p9bl - Eugene Berman / Shutterstock.com, p9br - Karolis Kavolelis / Shutterstock.com, p10bl - M.J.J. de Vaan / Shutterstock.com, p10br - Media_works / Shutterstock.com, p12tr - United States Air Force - The California State Military Museum http://www.militarymuseum.org/ImageLibrary.html, Public Domain, https://commons.wikimedia.org/w/index.php?curid=23169715, p12br - InsectWorld / Shutterstock.com, p12bl - VanderWolf Images / Shutterstock.com, p13tl - HoHun - de.wikipedia.org, CC BY-SA 3.0, https://commons.wikimedia.org/w/index.php?curid=450119, p13tm - Ala_delta.svg: Sorrunoderivative work: Steelpillow (talk) - Ala_delta.svg, CC BY-SA 3.0, https://commons.wikimedia.org/w/index.php?curid=7712060, p13tr - Steelpillow - Own work, CC BY-SA 3.0, https://commons.wikimedia.org/w/index.php?curid=7768289, p13br - Herget Josef / Shutterstock.com, p14m - Peter R Foster IDMA / Shutterstock.com, p14br - Arjan van de Logt / Shutterstock.com, p15m - NASA - http://antwrp.gsfc.nasa.gov/apod/ap040329.html [1]Catalogue: http://www.dfrc.nasa.gov/Gallery/Photo/X-43A/HTML/ED99-45243-01.htmlTransferred from en.wikipedia to Commons by TheDJ using CommonsHelper., Public Domain, https://commons.wikimedia.org/w/index.php?curid=4229854, p15bl - Leonid Faerberg (transport-photo.com) (GFDL 1.2 or GFDL 1.2), via Wikimedia Commons, p15br - vaalaa / Shutterstock.com, p16tl - schusterbauer.com / Shutterstock.com, p17tl - Jose Luis Stephens / Shutterstock.com, p17m - Liner / Shutterstock.com, p17br - VanderWolf Images / Shutterstock.com, p18tr - Angel DiBilio / Shutterstock.com, p18br - Fasttailwind / Shutterstock.com, p19t - Fdoamerica - Own work, CC0, https://commons.wikimedia.org/w/index.php?curid=62648010, p19b - myphotobank.com.au / Shutterstock.com, p20tr - Sorbis / Shutterstock.com, p20m - vaalaa / Shutterstock.com, p20br - M101Studio / Shutterstock.com, p21t - BestPhotoPlus / Shutterstock.com, p21m - Dave Subelack from YYC, Canada - 747-8I (N6067E)Altair78, CC BY-SA 2.0, https://commons.wikimedia.org/w/index.php?curid=15686692, p21bl - fivetonine / Shutterstock.com, p21br - Christian Heinz / Shutterstock.com, p23br - Evan El-Amin / Shutterstock.com, p24bl - ZRyzner / Shutterstock.com, p24br - Everett Collection / Shutterstock.com, p25tl - Rawpixel.com / Shutterstock.com, p25br - Matthew Simantov from Seattle, WA, USA, CC BY 2.0, via Wikimedia Commons, p30b - Ryan Fletcher / Shutterstock.com, p31ml - Yasir Nur Hidayat / Shutterstock.com

A catalogue record for this book is available from the National Library of Australia

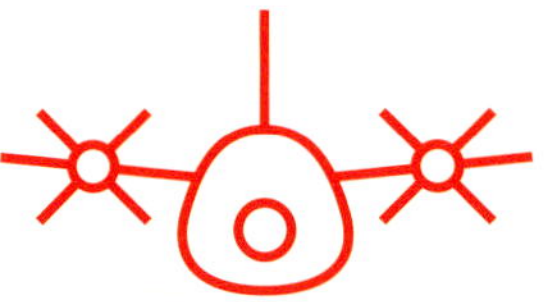

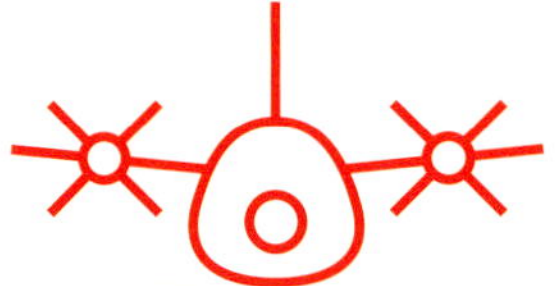

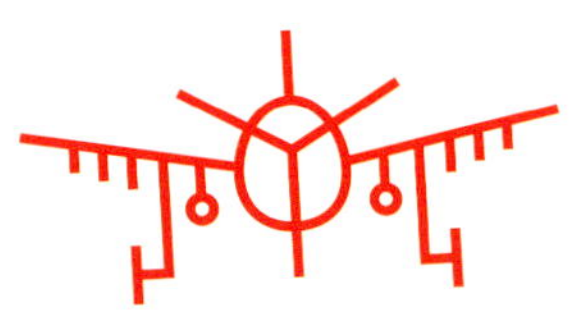

CONTENTS

How Do Planes Fly?

FORCES IN FLIGHT

The upward and forward forces in flight have opposing forces that work to stop them. Upward lift is opposed by gravity, and forward motion is opposed by drag, which wants to stop the aircraft moving forward.

The design of every aircraft has to take these four forces into consideration.

Aircraft fly using thrust and lift. Thrust comes from the engine and lift comes from the shape of the wing.

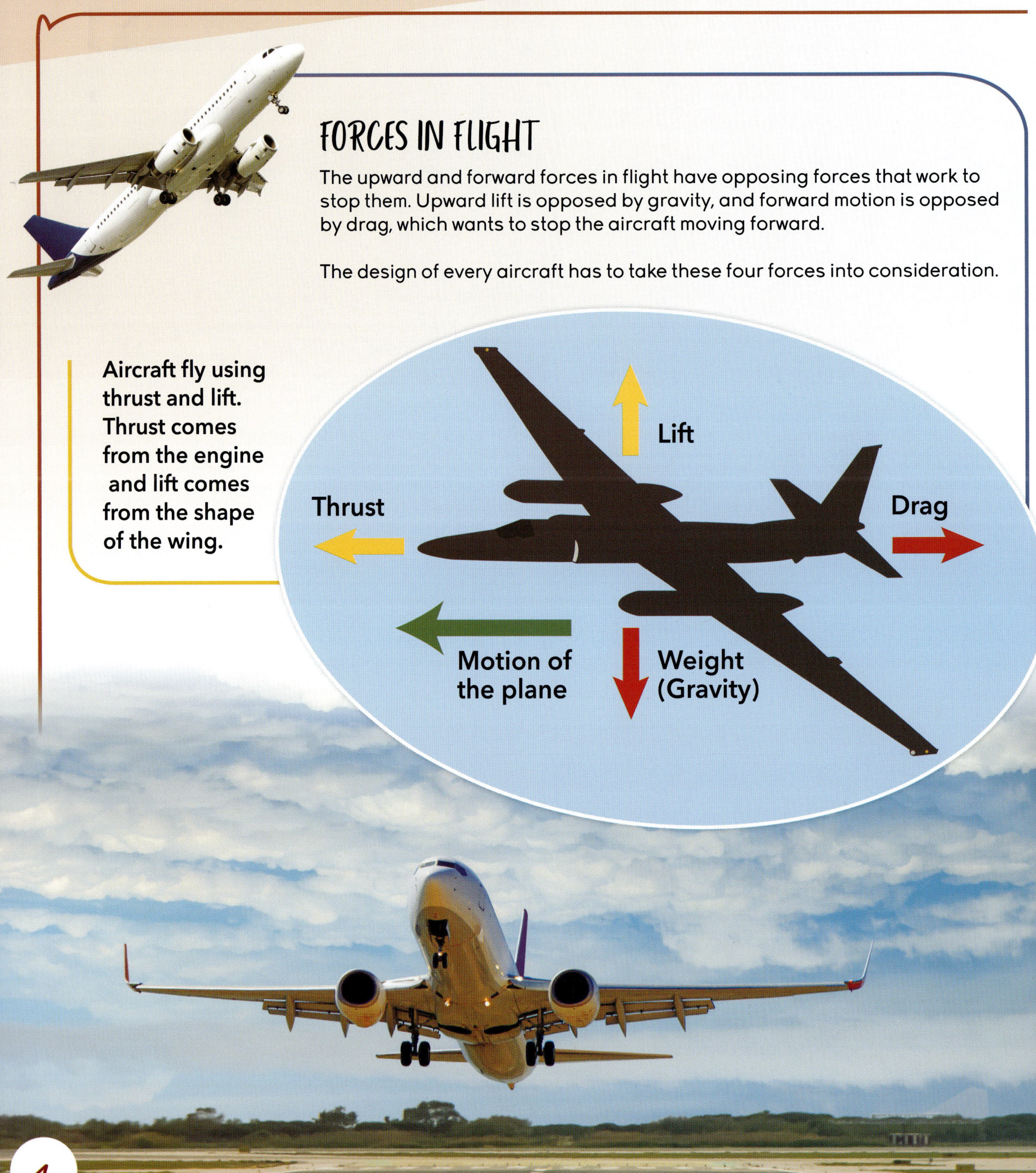

AEROFOIL

The wing shape of an aircraft that creates lift is called an aerofoil. It is curved on the upper surface and flatter underneath. This is the same shape that birds' wings have.

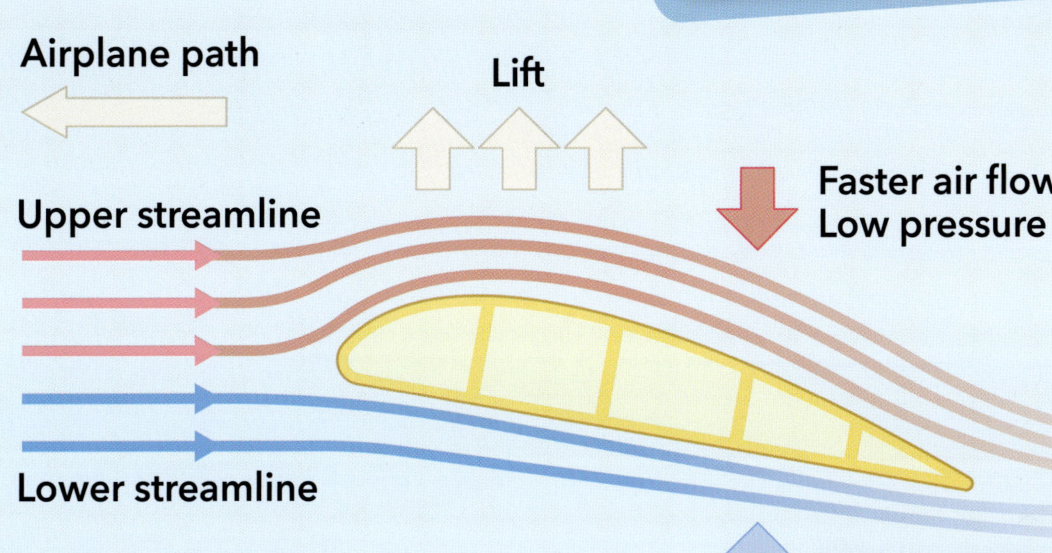

HOW IT WORKS

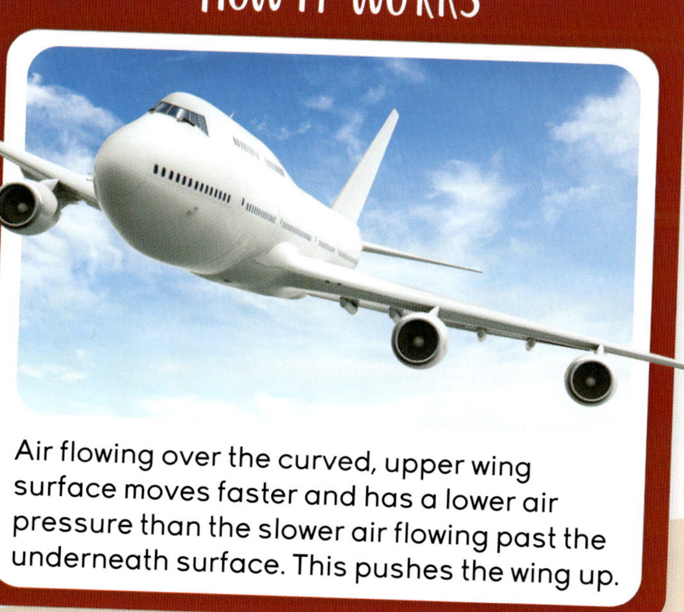

Air flowing over the curved, upper wing surface moves faster and has a lower air pressure than the slower air flowing past the underneath surface. This pushes the wing up.

Aircraft Engines

There are different sorts of aircraft engines, depending on the size, weight and usage of the aircraft.

JET ENGINES

Jet engines work by emitting a high-speed thrust of hot gas. This creates the forward motion of the aircraft.

TURBOJETS

A turbojet is a type of jet engine in which the gas is drawn into the engine and compressed. The compressed air is then used to make the fuel combust or burn.

RAMJETS AND SCRAMJETS

These forms of jet engines work at supersonic speeds. Ramjet engines are so fast they are used in missiles as well as fighter planes.

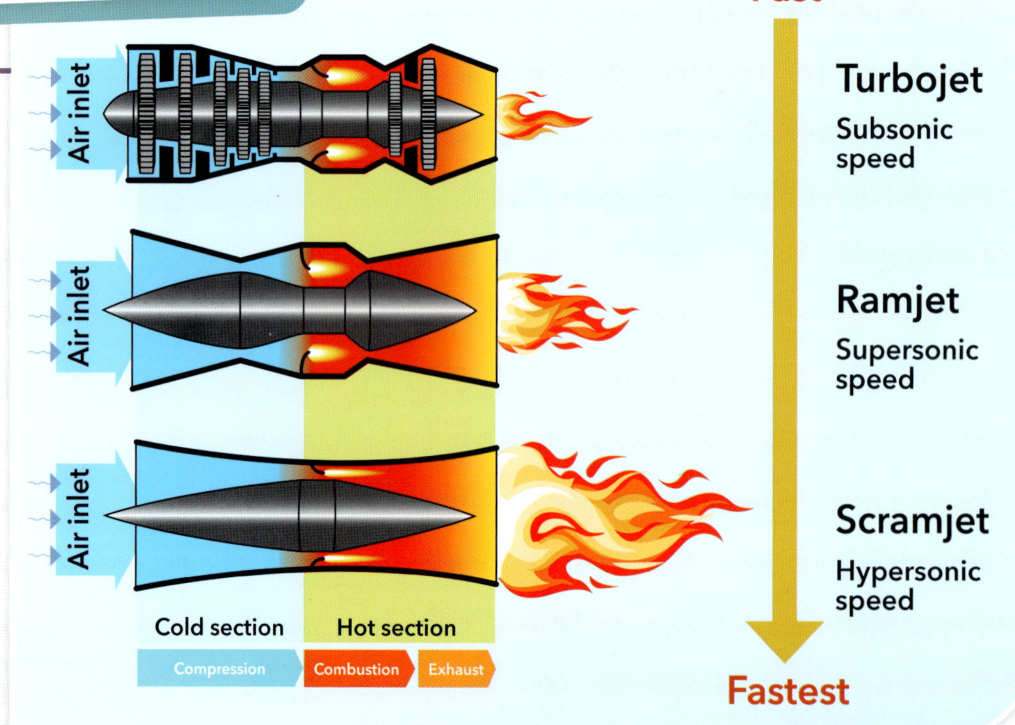

HELICOPTERS

A helicopter usually has a combustion engine. This engine powers the machinery which makes the blades of a helicopter turn.

LIGHT AIRPLANES

Light airplanes with turning propellers use combustion engines to create the turning movement.

GLIDERS

Gliders do not have engines. They rely on rising warm air currents, called thermals. Their long, thin wings help them to stay up in the air.

Bombers

A bomber is a military aircraft whose purpose is to drop bombs or release missiles.

XI'AN H-6K BOMBER

China's Xi'an H-6K bomber carries missiles that it launches from underneath each wing.

B-52 BOMBER

The USA's B-52 bombers have been in service for decades. They are large and heavy bombers that can carry a variety of weapons. Modern updates to the B-52 enable it to use guided missile technology.

B-21 RAIDER

The B-21 Raider is being developed to eventually replace the B-52 bombers. It may also act as an interceptor in the air, as well as being used to gather intelligence about enemy activities.

STEALTH BOMBER

The stealth bomber is a US Air Force aircraft. Stealth bombers are designed to hide from radars so that an enemy does not know they are in the air.

In the air, it looks like a black V-shape

ROCKWELL B-1 LANCER

The Rockwell B-1 Lancer is a supersonic bomber with wings that can change position during flight.

Part of the USA's fleet of bombers, the B-1 is unusual in having both supersonic speed and the ability to carry heavy missile loads.

Helicopters

A helicopter can land vertically in a small area, and take off again very quickly.

ENGINES

Most helicopters have turboshaft engines. These produce a rotating movement, rather than pushing gases out the back of the engine like turbojets.

ROTOR

Helicopters have one or more rotors. These include the blades and the machinery that turns them. Most helicopters have from two to seven blades in the rotor assembly.

AgustaWestland AW109, a lightweight twin-engine military helicopter.

WEIGHT

The heaviest helicopters weigh over 20 tonnes, but there are also very small, lightweight helicopters.

Russia's Mil Mi-26 helicopter is one of the heaviest helicopters ever constructed.

BLADES

Helicopter blades have the same curved aerofoil shape as fixed-wing airplanes. The blades provide lift by spinning, rather than by being pushed forward through the air.

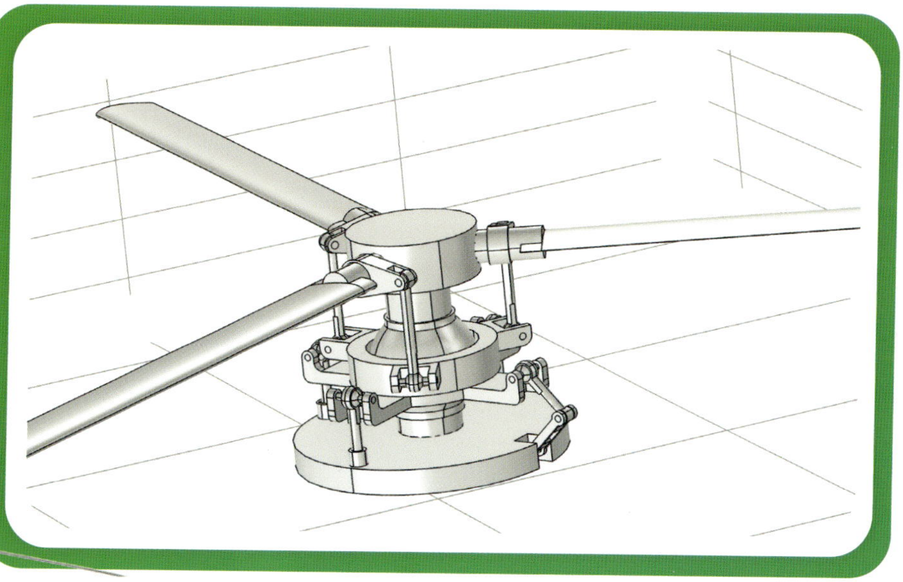

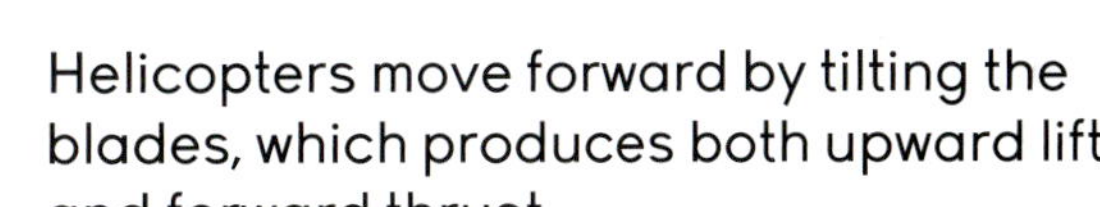

Helicopters move forward by tilting the blades, which produces both upward lift and forward thrust.

NICKNAMES

Helicopters are also called choppers, whirlybirds or copters.

CH-47F Chinook army helicopter

Delta Wing Aircraft

The delta-shaped wing is the one most often found on supersonic aircraft.

DELTA OR STRAIGHT?

A delta wing is a wing shaped in the form of a triangle. The straight wing, which gliders have, enables low-speed aircraft flight, but as the possible speed of an aircraft increases, the wing shape that allows the highest supersonic speed is the delta shape.

Examples of delta wing aircraft include the Mikoyan-Gurevich MiG-21, the Dassault Mirage 2000, the Eurofighter and most stealth fighter jets.

WHY IS IT CALLED DELTA?

The delta wing gets its name from the Greek uppercase letter 'delta', which shares the same triangular shape.

Mikoyan-Gurevich MiG-21

Dassault Mirage 2000

Eurofighter

Sweden's Saab 35 Draken has a tailless double-delta design.

NO TAIL

There are various designs for the delta wing aircraft, with the most extreme having no tail to the plane at all. The wing extends all the way to the rear of the body.

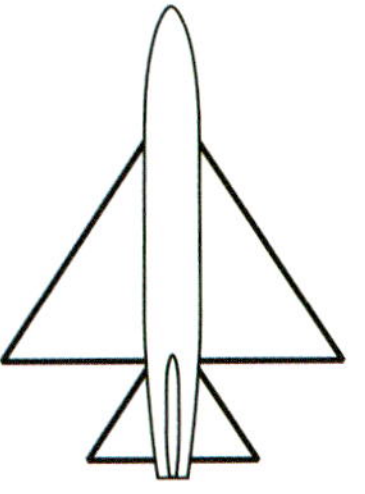

Tailed delta

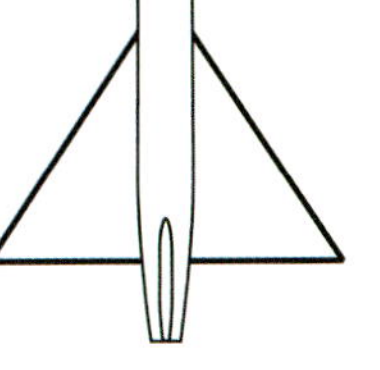

Tailless delta

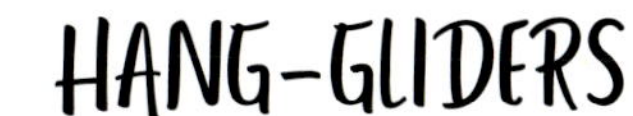

HANG-GLIDERS

Some hang-gliders also have a delta wing, taking the usefulness of this wing shape from national defence to fun flying.

CONCORDE

The Concorde was a passenger delta wing aircraft of the late 1900s. Its last flight was in 2003.

Fighter Jets

Jet aircraft can fly very fast using powerful engines that push large amounts of air backwards. This makes the aircraft move forward.

Fighter jets are small, fast and deadly. The pilots train so they can attack and defend, using advanced weapons and flight controls.

SONIC BOOM

A fighter jet going overhead makes a loud, booming noise. This 'sonic boom' comes from the compressed air around it as it flies faster than the speed of sound.

SPEED

A fighter jet flies at over 2,000 km/h (over 1,000 knots). This is supersonic, or faster than the speed of sound, which is 1,235 km/h.

X-43A

NASA's X-43A scramjet aircraft has flown at nearly Mach 10, which is ten times the speed of sound.

MiG-25

Some of the fastest jet planes in the world were the Soviet MiG-25 aircraft.

Cargo Aircraft

Cargo aircraft carry freight instead of passengers.

When you buy something from an online shop overseas and it is delivered quickly to your door, this is because a cargo plane has carried it. Over a third of the value of world trade depends on transport by cargo aircraft.

Some cargo aircraft have ramps at the back for loading large and heavy equipment. Inside the plane, all the cargo has to be tied down tightly.

Cargo aircraft usually have wide bodies to enable them to carry as much freight as possible. They may need extra wheels to support the weight of the cargo.

Many passenger aircraft reserve space in the cargo hold for carrying freight.

ANTONOV AN-225 MRIYA

The world's largest cargo aircraft was the Antonov AN-225 Mriya. It was destroyed in 2022 during the war between Ukraine and Russia.

DEFENCE FORCE CARGO

Defence forces need a lot of equipment delivered to them so they can do their jobs. Huge aircraft can carry tanks, helicopters, troops, food, weapons and more to wherever the men and women in the defence forces are located.

Passenger Aircraft

A business that operates passenger aircraft is called an airline.

Aircraft are broadly divided into two groups: military aircraft and civil aircraft. Civil aircraft means aircraft used for private and business use.

AIRLINES

Airlines operate services using aircraft that range in size. These planes might be small and have a single engine, or they could be large and extremely expensive to acquire and maintain.

PILOTS

Civil aviation pilots undergo extensive training before they can take an airplane full of passengers into the sky. They also have to do frequent top-up training, as well as health checks.

FLAG CARRIER

The term 'flag carrier' refers to a civil airline which is either run by the government of a country, or is in some other way a symbol of a country.

Air Marshall Islands is an airline that operates with a fleet of small aircraft.

SMALLEST AIRLINES

In remote areas, a small airline might operate only one or two, small aircraft. In some cases, these might be the only transport to the remote areas of a country, apart from hiking through a forest or jungle.

ROYAL FLYING DOCTOR

In Outback Australia, the Royal Flying Doctor Service provides medical help for people living in isolated places out in the bush. They have small planes and helicopters in their fleet.

Airbus and Boeing

Airbus and Boeing have the world's largest passenger aircraft.

The A380 Airbus is a large and very comfortable passenger aircraft. As the biggest passenger plane in the world, the A380-800 can carry 525 passengers seated in three classes.

The range for the Airbus is 14,800 kilometres (9,200 miles).

Each Airbus has four turbofan engines, made by either Rolls-Royce or Engine Alliance.

First class in an Airbus includes a private space, a bed and access to a shower.

BOEING 747-8

This aircraft can carry 467 passengers seated in three classes.

Turbofan engines power the Boeing 747.

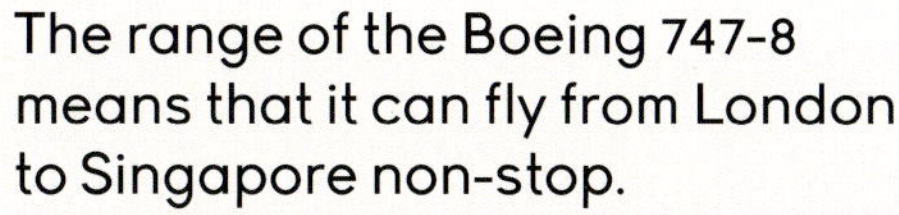

The range of the Boeing 747-8 means that it can fly from London to Singapore non-stop.

First class in the Boeing 747 includes a bed and a separated seating area for each passenger.

Private Jets

Private jets fly passengers around the world just like big airlines, but with more privacy, fewer passengers and with timetables that can be changed to suit the passengers' needs.

WHY HAVE PRIVATE JETS?

People fly in private jets when they want to be alone or just with their family and friends in the sky.

Countries have private jets so their leaders can fly in safety, and celebrities use private jets to avoid crowds of fans at airports.

ADVANTAGES

Private jets have a lot of room, and passengers can choose their own times to fly, rather than depending on the timetables of large airlines. A private jet can use smaller airports than the large, public airlines.

DISADVANTAGES

Private jets are very expensive to buy, maintain and even just to use as a passenger. They are harmful to the environment because they use more fuel per passenger, fly less efficiently, and add to noise and climate pollution.

THE MOST EXPENSIVE

Some of the most expensive private jets are:

- Air Force One (name given to the private jet when used by the President of the United States)
- Gulfstream III
- Bombardier Global 7000

Space Shuttle

The first space shuttle was launched by NASA in 1981.

For 30 years, the space shuttles carried astronauts and cargo to and from the International Space Station (ISS) in orbit around Earth. The space shuttles were named Atlantis, Challenger, Columbia, Discovery, Endeavour and Enterprise. Together they conducted 135 missions and carried 355 people.

DISASTERS

In 1986, Challenger broke apart 73 seconds after take-off. All seven crew members were killed. In 2003, Columbia broke apart on re-entry, resulting in the deaths of the seven astronauts on board.

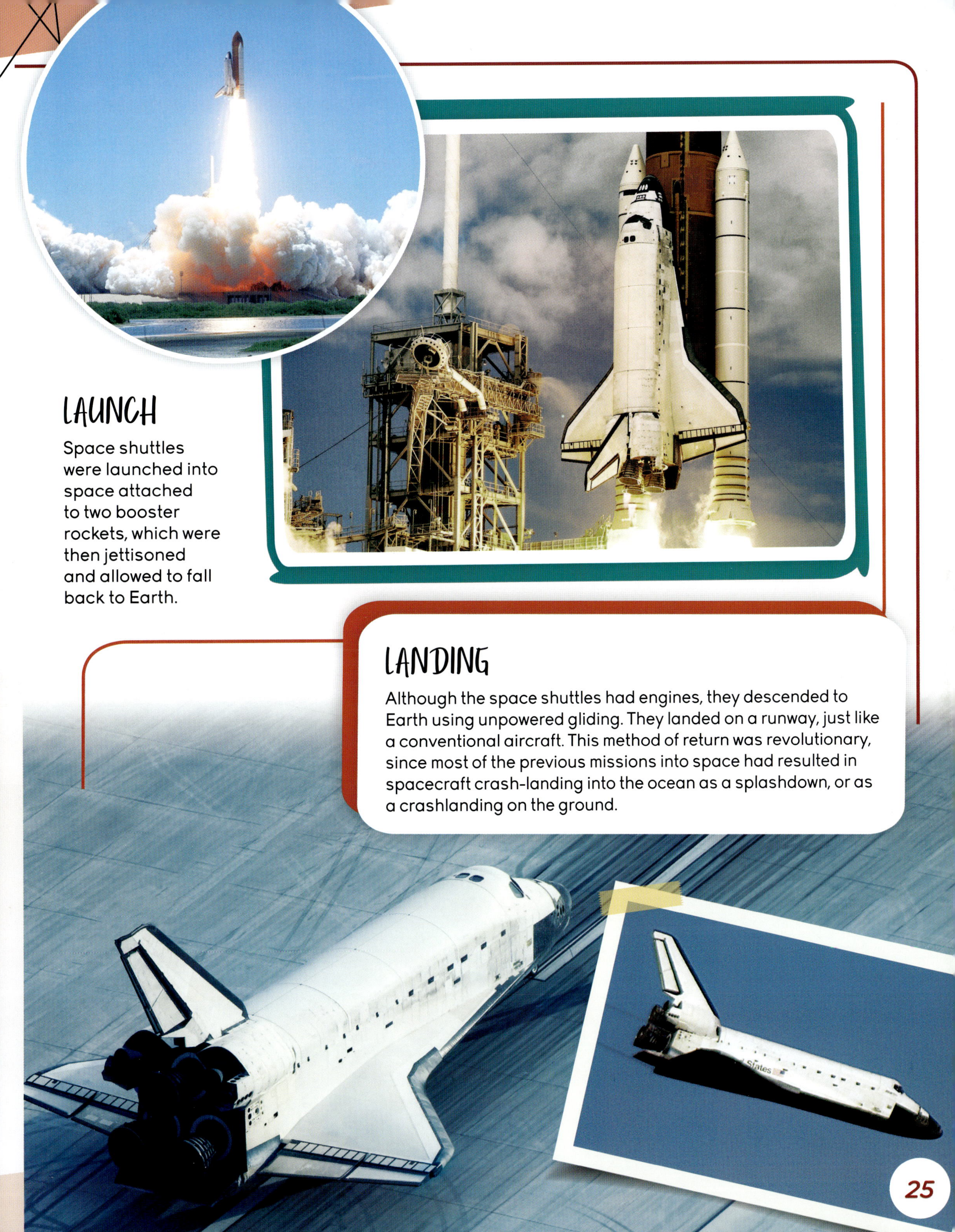

LAUNCH

Space shuttles were launched into space attached to two booster rockets, which were then jettisoned and allowed to fall back to Earth.

LANDING

Although the space shuttles had engines, they descended to Earth using unpowered gliding. They landed on a runway, just like a conventional aircraft. This method of return was revolutionary, since most of the previous missions into space had resulted in spacecraft crash-landing into the ocean as a splashdown, or as a crashlanding on the ground.

Drones

A drone is an uncrewed aircraft that is controlled by operators on the ground.

MILITARY DRONES

Uncrewed aerial drones are used for gathering information from the air, and some also carry missiles or bombs. Since there is no pilot safety to consider, these aircraft can be smaller, lighter and cheaper to make than other types. They range in size from small drones to larger aircraft, depending on how much weight they have to carry.

RECREATIONAL DRONES

With drones becoming smaller and cheaper, their use for recreation has increased. Many countries have laws about where a user can fly their drone. This protects the privacy of people on the ground, and stops drones from interfering with other aircraft.

WARFARE

Drones have become vital in modern warfare. They are used to gather intelligence about the enemy, and also to deploy explosives. Drones have been used by both sides in the Ukraine/Russia war.

DRONES AND INDUSTRY

Drones have changed the way people in many industries gather information:

- Drone photography helps advertise properties for sale
- Drones can search for people missing at sea or in dense forests
- Farmers use drones to check on their livestock and crops
- Drones can view and check on the condition of a structure during a building inspection
- Drones may be used for delivery services in the future

Gliders

Gliders are aircraft without an engine to power them through the air and provide forward thrust.

Gliders do not have an engine but they still manage to stay up in the air. The pilot achieves this by relying on rising currents of hot air. These are called thermals.

Gliders need to be made from lightweight material, such as fibreglass. Unlike hang-gliders or paragliders, fixed-wing gliders have a firm wing shape, which is long and narrow.

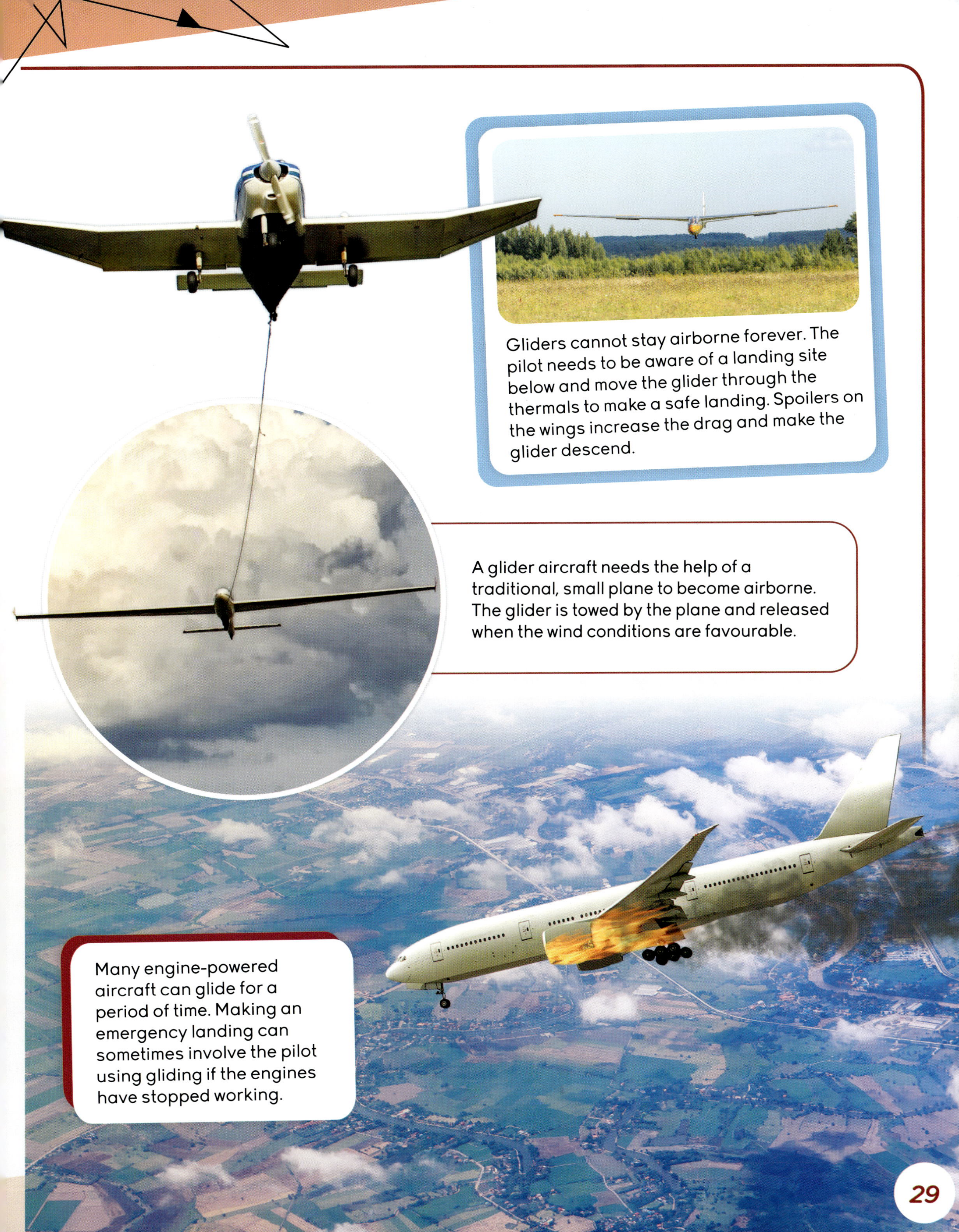

Gliders cannot stay airborne forever. The pilot needs to be aware of a landing site below and move the glider through the thermals to make a safe landing. Spoilers on the wings increase the drag and make the glider descend.

A glider aircraft needs the help of a traditional, small plane to become airborne. The glider is towed by the plane and released when the wind conditions are favourable.

Many engine-powered aircraft can glide for a period of time. Making an emergency landing can sometimes involve the pilot using gliding if the engines have stopped working.

Ultralights

Ultralights are small aircraft often used for recreational flying.

Ultralight aircraft usually carry no more than two passengers, and have small combustion or electric engines. Some of these aircraft are so light that a pilot can alter direction by shifting their body weight in the seat.

Ultralights bridge the gap between hang-gliding and powered flight.

Ultralights include powered hang-gliders, ultralight trikes, gyrocopters and small fixed-wing aircraft.

Ultralight aircraft are sometimes used by farmers in countries where farm sizes are very large. In these locations, using an ultralight is a practical way of getting from one part of the farm to another, particularly during times of flood when there may be no road access at all.

Glossary

aerofoil curved shape of a wing

intelligence (military) information obtained by spying

radar visual method of locating objects using radio waves

rotor blades and spinning machinery of a helicopter

sonic boom loud sound heard on the ground when an aircraft travels faster than sound

spoiler moveable sections of a wing that are used to reduce lift

supersonic faster than sound

thermals rising currents of warm air

thrust forward force

Index

U.S. POSTAGE
5¢
VIA AIR MAIL
U.S. POSTAGE
5¢
VIA AIR MAIL
BY AIR MAIL
PAR AVION